THE BLIND GIRL.

FRANCES JANE CROSBY

From Daguerreotype by Morand.

BLIND GIRL,

And Other Poems.

BY FRANCES JANE CROSBY,

A PUPIL AT THE

NEW-YORK INSTITUTION FOR THE BLIND.

————"Who best
Bears his mild yoke, they serve him best; his state
Is kingly." . . . MILTON.

NEW-YORK,
PUBLISHED BY WILEY & PUTNAM,
161 Broadway.
1844.

162413

PIERCY AND REED, PRINTERS,
9 Spruce-Street.

CONTENTS.

Preface 7

Dedication..11

The Blind Girl...13

The Rise and Progress.......................................20

Dedication of the Chapel....................................27

To the Senate of the State..................................29

The Blind Girl's Lament.....................................31

The Desolate..33

To the Heroes of Bunker Hill...............................36

Reflections on the Closing Year.............................38

The Captive...39

Thoughts at Midnight..42

Niagara...46

To an Absent Daughter.......................................47

To a Boquet...48

I'll Think of Thee (a song).................................50

On Receiving a Boquet.......................................51

Song of the Greek Girl......................................52

On the Death of a Parent....................................53

The Sleeping Infant...54

On the Death of the Father of a Fellow Pupil.........56

To a Friend and Fellow Pupil...............................58

Address to Miss D.................................60

The Orphan's Prayer.............................62

The Wish.......................................64

The Mandan Chief...............................65

Impromptu......................................67

On the Death of H. B...........................69

Easter Sunday...................................71

On the Death of a Child........................73

The Neglected Child............................75

"Jesus Wept"...................................78

Erin...79

"My Native Land"...............................82

The Emigrant...................................84

Address to Rev. Dr. Hewitt....................86

An Epithalamium................................88

"Speed Me to My Home"..........................90

The Guitar.....................................92

To a Spirit....................................94

Impromptu......................................96

Address to General Bertrand...................96

Requiem on Gen. Bertrand......................98

On the Departure of a Teacher.................100

To a Favorite Willow..........................101

To a Star.....................................103

Farewell to the Summer Flowers................105

On the Departure of a Pupil...................106

The Grecian War Song..........................107

Childhood.....................................108

Ode on the Fourth of July.....................109

Lines Addressed to C. B., Esq........................110
" My Prairie Home"................................101
Geneva...113
Solitude...115
On the Death of General Harrison.................116
Lament of Mrs. Harrison..........................118
On the Death of the Hon. H. S. Legare............120
The Sister's Lament..............................122
" They are Gone".................................124
To Lake Erie.....................................125
To a Favorite Plant..............................126
A Rose...127
The Tear...129
Reflections after a Drive........................130
Lines inscribed to Professor R...................132
My Mother's Grave................................134
Ida..134
Psalm iv. 8......................................139
The Christmas Hymn...............................140
To Solitude......................................141
The Blind Girl's Song............................143
" Shall I Meet Thee Again?"......................144
Jerusalem..145
Address delivered at the New York Tabernacle.....147
Address delivered before Congress................149
Address delivered before the Legislature of N. Jersey...152
An Address recited while on the Tour in 1842.....155
An Address recited while on the Tour in 1843.....158

PREFACE.

In venturing the publication of the little volume containing the poetic effusions of one, circumstanced as the authoress is, great reliance is placed on the forbearing spirit of those who may bestow on it a perusal; but the friends, by whose advice it is now presented for the patronage of the public, feel that partiality does not altogether forestal judgment, when they say, that apart from other considerations, the following productions are fraught with much that entitles them to that reception, which a sympathetic spirit might alone dictate.

Those who have listened to the occasional recitations of the authoress, when appeals have been made before the public, either in behalf of the Institution of which she has for nine years been an inmate, or of those who, like herself, in early life were deprived of mental, as well as natural light, will recollect the emotions excited by the touching strains in which the advantages she there enjoyed were pourtrayed; and while the tear gathered in the eye, have experienced a higher sense of gratitude for the possession of that blessing, of which she, with those around her, were deprived.

That one, who from the earliest period of infancy has been deprived of sight, and whose entire knowledge of external objects, from which to paint with the imagination's pencil, has been derived from oral description, should be able thus faithfully to present scenes from nature, and in colors so vivid and true, as to render the reader incredulous as to the originality of the production, is a subject of surprise, as well as admiration. This, however, is a striking evidence of the effect of the culturing hand of education on this class of our unfortunate fellow-citizens, and none higher or more conclusive could be given, of the utility of that system, which has produced such happy results on her, and others like her, who have found an intellectual recompense within the walls of those Institutions, where it is so effectually brought to bear.

It is generally, and correctly believed, that the minds of those whose thoughts are not distracted by external objects, are capable of greater concentration, but it is not the less important that culture should open the avenue to thought, otherwise it must roam round its prison house, chafed with ideas indistinct and unsatisfactory, struggling for escape from a chaotic existence. The present age has felt the full force of this, and enlightened counsels have legislated most effectually to secure to this class and those deprived of the sense of hearing, means by which alone they can be efficiently instructed in *all* the branches of education. Thus we find among the sightless, those who expatiate on "the glory of the moon and the stars which He has made," and among the mute those who unfold the mysteries of revelation.

Frances Jane Crosby, whose compositions are to be found in the following pages, was deprived of sight by illness at the early age of six weeks. She entered "*The New-York Institution for the Blind*" when she was fifteen years old, prior to which her opportunities for education were exceedingly limited ; losing her father in her infancy, her remaining parent was left in indigent circumstances, to provide for herself, and therefore unable to bestow that care on her sightless daughter, which she so much needed.

Thus the dawn of her mental existence may be said to have commenced with her introduction to the Institution, from which period her intellectual powers have expanded, until her imaginative mind has been enabled to clothe its thoughts in language at once chaste and poetic.

Whatever merit the public may accord to these effusions, most of which were addressed to personal friends as occasioned by the incidents to which they refer, and were not designed for the press ; it may rest assured that the several pieces are the unaided productions of the authoress. They were penned from dictation, with very little revision by herself, and less from any other source. Thus in many instances much of the spirit of the composition may have been lost by punctuation, which had it been done by the composer, would convey more justly the thought intended.

With these prefatory remarks, the book is thrown into that prolific tide, which now flows from that vast machine "the Press," hardly venturing to hope, that amidst its teeming productions, much pecuniary advantage will be realized to "THE BLIND GIRL," for whose benefit it is published, and whose declining health renders its avails the more important.

It is however believed, that a feeling, kindred to that which prompts the writer to the present publication, will influence those to whom it is now offered.

April, 1844.

DEDICATION.

Since those whose judgment I esteem
　　Superior to my own,
These scattered thoughts, which have employed
　　My leisure hours alone,
Advise, that to the public eye
　　They should presented be ;
Though such a step, till counselled thus,
　　Had ne'er occurred to me :
The course, which author's have pursued,
　　I too would imitate,
And to some valued friend or friends
　　This work would dedicate.

Whom should I more revere than those,
　　Who o'er my youthful hours,
Have long the faithful guardians been,
　　And strewed my path with flowers ?
But language how inadequate
　　Their kindness to express !
Yet God's all-seeing eye beholds—
　　And will that kindness bless.
This feeble token of esteem,
　　Dear friends, to you I bring ;
Accept the grateful tribute, then—
　　" Affection's offering."

　　　　　　　　　　　　F. J. C.

THE BLIND GIRL.

HER home was near an ancient wood,
Where many an oak gigantic stood,
And fragrant flowers of every hue
In that sequestered valley grew—
   A church there reared its little spire ;
And in their neat and plain attire,
The humble peasants would repair
On Sabbath morn, to worship there ;
   And on the laughing breeze would float
The merry warbler's choral note,
When at Aurora's rosy dawn,
She decked with light the dewy lawn.
   A pearly stream meander'd there ;
And on its verdant banks so fair,
From school released, at close of day,
A group of happy girls would play.
   With their gay laugh the woodlands rang ;
Or if some rustic air they sang,
Those rural notes, of music sweet,
Echo, would in mock tones repeat.

B

Amid those scenes of mirth and glee,
That sightless girl, oh where was she ?
Was she, too, blithely sporting there,
Or wreathing garlands for her hair ?
　　She sat beside her cottage door ;
Her brow a pensive sadness wore ;
And while she listened to the song
That issued from that youthful throng ;
　　The tears, warm gushing on her cheek,
Told what no language e'er could speak ;
While their young hearts were light and gay,
Her hours passed heavily away.—
　　A mental night was o'er her thrown ;
She sat dejected, and alone.
Yet, no ; a mother's accents dear,
Came softly on that blind girl's ear.
　　While all were locked in dreamy sleep,
That mother, o'er her couch would weep,
And as she knelt in silence there,
Would breathe to God her fervent prayer ;
　　" That He, all merciful and mild,
　　Would bless her sightless—only child."

'Twas eve—the summer's sky was bright,
The crescent moon unveiled her light,
And many a mild and radiant star
Its lustre spread o'er climes afar.

That mother, to her throbbing breast
Her lovely daughter fondly pressed,
She on her bosom leaned her head,
And thus in mournful accents said :
  " Tell me, dear mother, what is sight ?
I hear you say the stars are bright
In yonder sky of azure hue ;
I wish I could behold them, too :
  You tell me of the summer flowers,
That blossom in the green wood bowers,
Their balmy breath is sweet to me,
And shall I ne'er their beauty see ?"
  There Anna paused—her mother sighed,
Then in a low, sweet voice, replied :
" On *earth* these joys may ne'er be thine,
But why, my child, *why* thus repine !
  'Tis thy Almighty Father's will,
He bids thy murmuring heart be still ;
There is a fairer world than this—
A world of never-fading bliss.
There let thy heart—thy treasure be,
And thou its purer joys shalt see."

  The summer and the autumn passed,
And wildly blew the winter blast ;
'Twas midnight, nature slept profound,
Unbroken stillness reigned around—

Save in one little cottage, where
Was heard a dying mother's prayer.
  "Oh God, my helpless orphan see,
She hath no other friend but Thee;
She frendless on the world is thrown
Sightless—heart-broken—and alone ;—
Father all merciful and mild—
Oh God ! protect my orphan child !"
  One last farewell that mother breathed—
One parting sigh her bosom heaved,
And all was over—she had fled
To mingle with the silent dead.

  The dreary winter passed away,
The spring returned and all was gay;
O'er hill and vale, and verdant plain,
The warbling choir was heard again.
  Yet spring or nature's cheerful voice,
Made not that orphan's heart rejoice;
Her mother's grave was near her cot,
And Anna, to that lonely spot
Led by some friendly hand, would stray,
To kiss the turf that wrapt her clay.

  'Twas evening's melancholy hour,
And zephyrs fanned each sleeping flower ;
O'er her soft lute her fingers ran,
And thus her mournful lay began :

"Alas! how bitter is my lot,
Without a friend—without a home—
Alone—unpitied and forgot—
A sightless orphan, now I roam.
Where is that gentle mother now,
Who once so fondly o'er me smiled,
Who gently kissed my burning brow,
And to her bosom clasped her child?
I could not see that angel eye,
Suffused with many a bitter tear,
But oh! her deep, heart-rending sigh,
Stole mournful on my listening ear.
I knelt beside her dying bed,
I felt her last expiring breath,
God bless my child, she faintly said,
And closed those lovely eyes in death.
Oh! how I long to soar away,
Where that departed one doth dwell,
To join with her the choral lay,
Angelic choirs forever swell!"

She ceased—she heard a footstep near,
A voice broke gently on her ear:
"Maiden, I've heard thy tale of woe,
And more of thee I fain would know;
Oh tell me why thy youthful brow
Is mantled o'er with sadness now?"
"Sir," she replied, "well may I weep;
Beneath this little mound, doth sleep

B*

All that on earth to me was dear;
My mother's lifeless form lies here;
And I, her only child, am left
Of kindred, and of home bereft;
But He who marks the sparrow's fall,
Will hear the helpless orphan's call.
My mother *bid* me trust His care,
He will not leave me to despair."
    The stranger sighed; "Maiden," said he,
" Thou hast my warmest sympathy;
No longer friendless shalt thou roam,
I'll take thee to a happier home;
A home erected for the Blind—
Where friends, affectionate and kind,
Will o'er thee watch with tender care,
And wipe away the orphan's tear."
" Forgive me, sir!" the maiden said,
As modestly she bent her head;
" I cannot bear to leave this grave,
Where these pale flowers so sadly wave,
And oh! while here I sit alone,
And listen to the wind's low moan,
Methinks my sainted mother dear
Smiles on me from her starry sphere,
And softly then she seems to say,
' My child, my darling, come away
To the bright mansion where I dwell,
And bid that world of care farewell."

The stranger wept; his generous heart
In other's sorrows shared a part.
" Thou must not linger here," said he,
" Haste, I entreat thee, haste with me,
Thou lone one, to that dear retreat,
Where thou a sister band shalt meet ;
Yes, maiden, they are *blind*, like thee,
And they will love thee tenderly."

How changed! that sightless orphan now :
No longer clouded is her brow ;
Her buoyant step is light and free,
And none more happy is than she :
For *Education's* glorious light
Hath chased away her mental night.
Contentment smiles upon her face,
And with delight, her fingers trace
The page, " by inspiration given,"
To guide her to a brighter heaven.
If o'er the past her memory stray,
Then *music's* sweet and charming lay,
Drives each dark vision from her breast,
And lulls each heaving sigh to rest.
Her grateful lips breathe many a prayer
For him who kindly placed her there.

[The foregoing was suggested by an incident which occurred
while visiting the interior of the State of New York, with a view
of satisfying the public mind of the advantages to be derived
from placing the blind at the Institution, and was inscribed to
H. M., one of the managers, who accompanied the party, without reference to publication.]

THE RISE AND PROGRESS

OF THE NEW YORK INSTITUTION FOR THE BLIND

COME, gentle muse ! my lay inspire ;
Once more I tune my slumbering lyre,
And fain would toûch its sweetest string ;
Aid me ! oh ! aid me, while I sing.
But say of what my song shall be ?
Would'st hear a *plaintive* melody ?
Or shall I wake a nobler strain—
Some warlike hero's deeds of fame ;
Or, borne on fancy's magic wing,
Fly to Castalia's limpid spring ;
Or climb Parnassus, and behold
Where gods and goddesses of old
Were wont, in fair Elysian bowers,
To dwell mid amaranthine flowers ;
Or sing of fair Columbia,
Our own bright land of liberty—
Where o'er full many a patriot's grave,
Doth freedom's spangled banner wave ?
I seek no dreams of fiction now,
Nor wreaths to deck a warrior's brow ;

The theme, my *happy home* shall be,
Endear'd by tenderest ties to me ;
Here many a rolling year has flown,
The brightest joys I e'er have known ;
Here have I felt—nor could my heart
Endure from scenes like these to part;
I cannot look o'er earth abroad,
And view the wondrous works of God—
The distant range of mountains high,
Whose snow-cap't summits reach the sky—
The landscape, in its robes of green—
The star-gem'd firmament serene ;
An all-wise providence Divine
Has this denied,—shall I repine ?
No ; to my heavenly Father's will,
I bow submissive, and be still.

Reader ! permit me to contrast
Our present prospects, with the past ;
And if this simple melody
Hath touch'd a chord of sympathy—
Tho' scarce I dare to hope, a strain
So humble, would thy notice claim,—
Go, gentle reader, back with me
A few short years, and thou shalt see
The blind, in mental darkness, left
Their way to grope, and many reft
Of all that rendered life most dear,
Without one beam of hope to cheer

Their stricken hearts ; ah ! they were thrown
Friendless, upon the world alone ;
Touch'd with compassion for their woes,
A philanthropic few arose,
Resolved the blind to educate,
And thus their lot ameliorate.

The period now my muse hath sung
To that of eighteen thirty-one.
Three sightless *orphans* they obtained,—
Their love, their confidence, they gained ;
The mental progress that was made,
Soon their instructor's toil repaid :
Thus weeks and months flew quickly by,
Until, at last the public eye
They by some presentations drew ;
For they could scarce believe it true,
That those on whom the orb of day
Had never shed its golden ray,
By touch alone, were taught to read ;
This seemed *impossible* indeed.

Their numbers rapidly increased,
And soon to them was kindly leased
A private mansion, and around,
Old trees o'erspread the pleasure ground.
Here first, upon *my* mental sight
Was poured instruction's dawning light,

Ere yet this stately pile was reared,
Which shall for ages stand rever'd ;
Close to this spot our home did stand,
And we were but a little band.
Our funds were small, our patrons few,
Still did our managers pursuo
Their arduous work, and many a year,
They struggled on, for hope was near ;
Tho' countless obstacles they met,
That radiant star smil'd on them yet.

Thus to our State they then applied,
Nor was their aid by it denied,
She did her fostering care bestow,—
What gratitude to her we owe !
How oft my wandering thoughts have stray'd
To when this corner-stone was laid :
'Twas winter, yet the day was mild,
And Nature on the structure smil'd ;
The prayers then offered, seemed to rise
Like holy incense to the skies ;
In lofty strains, a choral lay
Was wafted on the breeze away.
Quickly the dreary winter pass'd,
The gentle spring returned at last ;
Then rapidly the work progressed,
For God, from heaven beheld, and bless'd.
The summer came, and pass'd away,
And autumn, clad in its array

Of faded charms, each verdant hill;
The voice of winter loud and shrill,
Broke on our ear, with mournful sound,
And in its icy fetters bound,
The chrystal streams forbore to flow,
And Nature wore her garb of snow.
'Twas then, with heartfelt sorrow true,
We bade our much-lov'd home adieu ;
For oh ! its ancient walls had long
Resounded with our joyous song.
We saw it soon in ruin laid,
And e'en the willow, 'neath whose shade,
A circle nightly gathered round,
The woodman's axe hurled to the ground.

Thus time sped on with rapid flight :
Now, with emotions of delight,
This noble edifice, complete,
We view—and in its dear retreat,
The friendless, the deserted blind,
Thank heaven ! a home and friends do find.

Reader ! art weary of my lay ?
Or would'st our happy home survey ?
Come then—I'll thy conductor be,—
Enter its Gothic walls with me.
Mark yonder group—can'st thou not trace
A cheerful smile on every face,

As arm in arm, the spacious hall
They promenade, and *sightless* all—
Hark !—gently bursting on thine ear,
The voice of music, soft, and clear ;
Now mournfully, the cadence floats,
And now, it swells in loftier notes :
Methinks thou long could'st linger here,
But to the school-room we'll repair :
Here, for a moment, pause and view,
As each their various tasks pursue,
The unclouded brow, the glowing cheek,
Which doth the heart's own language speak ;
Let solemn awe inspire thy breast,
And in the sacred chapel rest—
Where, on each holy Sabbath day
We meet to praise our God and pray.
His ministers, of every name,
The Gospel messages proclaim ;
Nor do we worship here alone—
To all, our doors are open thrown—
Yes, all, who love the house of prayer,
We cordially invite them there.

Now fade the crimson tints of day,
The setting sun, its dying ray
Sheds softly from the purple west,
O'er the majestic Hudson's breast.

Oh ! gaze upon this magic scene,
The sky, all cloudless and serene ;
Onward that mighty river flows,
And Nature sinks to sweet repose ;
Well may a home like ours be dear :
Ah ! who could not be happy here ?
Sweet thought—the blind from every State
May in its joys participate !

And now, my muse ! farewell to thee—
Here would I close my melody,
And leave thee, gentle reader, too,
And breathe the parting word—adieu !

DEDICATION OF THE CHAPEL.

Oh ! thou omniscient, omnipresent Lord !
  Invisible, eternal God of all !
The vast creation trembles at thy word
  And at thy footstool nations prostrate fall.

Thy throne is fixed above the starry frame ;
  Yet thou, in earthly temples lov'st to dwell.
The humble spirit thou wilt not disdain—
  The wounded heart, thy balm divine dost heal.

Father, we humbly supplicate thy grace ;—
  May thy benignant smiles to us be given ;
Thy blessing rest upon this sacred place ;
  Thine earthly house—we trust, the gate of
    heaven.

Here will we listen to thy holy word ;
  Light to our path, oh ! may its precepts be ;
Here shall the voice of praise, and prayer be
    heard—
  Ourselves, our all, we dedicate to thee.

Protect, oh Lord! the dwelling of the blind,
  And to its guardians, aid divine impart;
Oh! make us to thy holy will resigned,
  Let love and union reign in every heart.

Accept our songs of gratitude and praise;
  Soon may we tune the golden lyres above,
And with cherubic legions, sweetly raise,
  The ceaseless anthems of eternal love.

SENATE OF THE STATE OF NEW YORK,

On the occasion of the Institution being visited by the Honorable the Senate of the State, sitting in New York as a Court for the Correction of Errors. *June* 22, 1843.

WARM hearted friends, we smile with you to meet,
We bid you welcome to our dear retreat ;
This stately pile a monument doth stand
Of your munificence, illustrious band !

Thanks to our State, we with one voice exclaim,
Her aid was not solicited in vain ;
To her, through your benevolence we owe
The calm delights that in our bosoms glow.

Yon glorious orb that gilds the azure skies,
Sheds not a ray to cheer these sightless eyes ;
The dewy lawn, mild nature's sylvan bowers,
To trace these lovely scenes must ne'er be ours.

c*

But education's pure refulgent light
Illumes our souls, dispels our mental night;
Joy on each brow a smiling garland weaves,
Here too, her magic strain soft music breathes.

Our gratitude, these lips may ne'er express,
Yet God above, your generous acts shall bless;
The page of hist'ry shall record your fame,
And thousands yet unborn, shall bless your name.

A few short years and we, who now are here,
Must bid farewell, the home to us so dear;
Yes, other forms beneath this roof will dwell,
And other lips shall of your kindness tell.

Adieu, for you our fervent prayers shall rise
To the Almighty Ruler of the skies,
Still shall your mem'ry round each heart be twin'd,
Adieu, ye friends and patrons of the Blind!

THE BLIND GIRL'S LAMENT.

AGAIN the well remembered spot I tread—
  The spot, of all on earth, most dear to me;
Ye scenes of childhood, now for ever fled,
  Fond memory brings you back, with all your
    glee.
When morn's fair goddess wide her gates did ope,
  I've wandered here, to greet her early dawn;
When tuneful b   heir melodies awoke,
  I've heard thy murmurs, lovely Horicon.*
But on the bosom of that stream to gaze,
  These sightless orbs, alas! now strive in vain;
The golden sun sheds not for me its rays,
  To light o'er once familiar scenes again.
Oh! what is sight? A gift I ne'er can know—
  But never let me murmur or repine.
Why should these eyes with tears of grief o'erflow,
  For that which never, never, can be mine?
Here have I roamed at twilight's pensive hour,
  When stars illum'd the blue ethereal sky;
Here breathed the fragrance of each sleeping
    flower,
  And heard the balmy zephyr's gentle sigh.

      * The Indian name for Lake George.

But where are those my bosom held so dear,
 Who in my joys and sorrows shared a part;
Whose accents fell like music on my ear!
 How sacred is their memory to my heart.
Alas! their dwelling is the stranger's home;
 I call, but echo's voice alone replies;
And as I wander o'er the spot, alone,
 Unbidden tears of grief suffuse my eyes.
When sorrow blights some fondly cherished
  flower
 We've nourished long, and tenderly caressed,
Is there a balm that in that cheerless hour
 Can sooth the anguish of the troubled breast?
Oh, yes! Hope fondly whispers in mine ear,
 That with those loved ones I shall meet again;
She from my cheek doth wipe the gushing tear,
 And bids my anxious heart no more complain.

THE DESOLATE.

Ah! why my heart so crushed and sad?
  Why fall these tears of anguish deep?
There's not a tone mine ear can glad,
  Oh! let me weep.

Why sleeps my lyre, why silent now,
  Those chords that once I lov'd to sweep?
A shade is gathering o'er my brow,
  Oh! let me weep.

Fair star of hope, celestial beam!
  Say hast thou set, forever set?
Thy smile was but a pleasing dream,
  I must forget.

The victim of distracting care,
  My isolated heart in vain
Would seek a kindred one to share,
  And lull its pain.

Oh, slander! On that guiltless name,
  Why thy reproaches basely heap?
Why innocence thus falsely blame?
  Oh! let me weep.

Though thou hast wronged the truest heart,
  That ever beat in mortal breast,
Each wound inflicted by thy dart,
  Shall be redressed.

'Tis evening; once my favorite hour;
  Pale Phœbus lights the crested deep;
But, oh! how lonely looks my bower,—
  Oh! let me weep.

The blushing rose its fragrance shed
  So sweetly on the balmy air,
The mignionette then raised its head,
  My tender care.

I saw them droop beneath the storms,
  That o'er my bower too rudely swept;
I knelt to kiss their withered forms,
  Then turned and wept.

Before me passed a youthful train;
  I heard their merry notes of glee;
Yet not one bosom could I claim,
  That beat for me.

E'en she, whose love I thought so true,
  Who 'round me clung so tenderly,
Whose tears would oft my cheek bedew,
  Was false to me.

I stood beside a limpid stream,
  Pure gushing from a rock-bound hill,
The air was bland; the sky serene;
  And all was still.

A trembling star, of mildest hue,
  Was gleaming in the purple west,
And pearly drops of balmy dew,
  Young flowers caressed.

Oh ! lovely orb, as the eye traced,
  Methinks thou to my memory,
Did'st paint a well remembered face,
  Once dear to me.

While thus I mused, a threatening cloud
  Swept o'er the sky of azure blue,
That radiant star, in its dark shroud,
  Sank from my view.

I gazed ; the cloud soon passed away,
  Again that star burst on mine eye ;
I felt a calm serenity,
  I knew not why.

When sorrow wrings my aching heart,
  And all is dead and drear to me,
Fair star ! thy lustre then impart—
  My guardian be.

TO THE HEROES OF BUNKER'S HILL.

REST, warriors, rest! your toils are o'er;
The war-drum beats to arms no more;
The thundering cannon's dreadful sound,
Shall never wake your sleep profound.

Rest, warriors, rest! while o'er your graves,
The tree you planted nobly waves;
This blood-stained field your deeds proclaim,
And victory's laurels crown your name.

Rest, warriors, rest! ye patriot band,
This stately monument shall stand;
Rear to the clouds its towering head,
When centuries their flight have sped.

Born to inhale pure freedom's air,
You scorn'd Britannia's yoke to wear;
By freedom's sacred rites you swore
To be a monarch's slaves no more.

Britannia heard, and soon a band
Of trusty warriors reach our land.
The morning dawned serene and bright,
And in the sun's resplendent light

Their armor gleams.   But what to you,
Is their display, ye gallant few ?
Fierce glances light the foeman's eye,
Your own with equal fire reply.

But hark ! the bugle's dread alarms
Now calls aloud, to arms ! to arms !
Quickly the signal ye obeyed,
Met the bold tyrant undismayed.

When bleeding on this spot you lay,
And life was ebbing fast away,
Still were your faithful voices heard—
" Fight, comrades, fight !" your dying word.

" Burst the stern chain of slavery—
Columbia, thou shalt yet be free."
And she is free, illustrious band !
Kind heaven hath smil'd upon our land.

REFLECTIONS ON THE CLOSING YEAR,
1843.

'Twill soon be gone—the wailing night wind drear
Chaunts her sad requiem to the closing year;
'Twill soon be gone—the brilliant starry train,
In silent eloquence repeat the strain.

'Twill soon be gone—the placid queen of night,
O'er its departure sheds her mellow light;
Oh, time! what art thou? who thy course may
   stay?
Not ours the past nor future, *but to-day.*

Hark! hark! the distant peal of yonder bell,
In measured tones the midnight hour doth tell—
Old year! thy reign is passed, we bid adieu
To thee, and smiling usher in the new.

I'll to my couch, and dream the hours away,
'Till fair Aurora opes the gates of day;
But e'er I go, dear friends, on you I call,
" A happy new year" is my wish to all.

THE CAPTIVE.

THE deep-toned bell, from Linder's lofty tower,
With awful peal proclaims the midnight hour ;
And spectres grim, in robes of ghastly white,
Come forth to wander 'mid the gloom of night.

They move with noiseless tread, that ghostly train,
Low, muttering sounds, convulse the trembling
    frame ;
The eye revolts in terror from the sight,
The blood congeals, the cheek grows deathly
    white.

That ancient tower, for centuries hath stood,
The scene of barbarous cruelty and blood :
The hapless victim, doom'd to torturing pain,
Though innocent, for mercy pleads in vain,
Within those hated walls her accents never came.

Blind superstition wields its sceptre there,
And fiends in human form its tenants are ;
The mangled wretch, with frantic joy they see,
And laugh exulting at his agony.

Within a deep and loathsome vault, confined
For years, a captive, hath Alvero pined ;
A youth of noble origin is he,
In this abode of guilt and misery.

Why is he doom'd a wretched life to spend ?
Oh, death to him would be a welcome friend ;
Pale and distorted are his features now,
And grief sits silent on his lofty brow.

Say, what his crime ? ask of that tyrant band
That with malignant looks around him stand ;
Fell murderers, hold ! ye stern, accursed throng,
Hold ! or high heaven will yet avenge his wrong.

'Tis done ! 'tis done ! I see the quivering dart,
The life-blood gushes from Alvero's heart,—
A deep convulsive sigh his bosom yields,
Hark ! hark ! methinks a kindred name he
        breathes.

" Oh, Eveline !—far, far from thee I die—
Would thou could'st hear my last expiring sigh ;
Would that my head were pillowed on thy breast,
How calm, how peaceful, could I sink to rest.

If those who dwell in yon celestial sphere,
Forget not those they lov'd on earth so dear;
If mortal's sorrows, they perchance may see,
My faithful spirit shall thy guardian be."

A groan—another—he has passed away,
To the bright regions of eternal day,
The affrighted raven screams and flaps her wings,
Night's mournful wind the captive's requiem sings.

THOUGHTS AT MIDNIGHT.

PALE Cynthia, lovely goddess of the night,
That o'er reposing nature sheds her light,
Ye radiant stars, that shine from pole to pole—
That round this dark terrestrial planet roll,

Fain would I to your distant regions soar,
And traverse worlds unseen—unknown before.
Oh ! restless spirit, would'st presume to scale
Those airy heights, or lift the mystic veil ?

Vain wish : aside that veil thou may'st not draw ;
It is not thine to scan creation's law ;
Study what God reveals, and ask no more,
And where thou can'st not comprehend, adore.

He to those countless orbs has lustre given ;
His hand directs them through the pathless
          heaven ;
He at a glance the universe surveys—
Deep and incomprehensible his ways.

But hark ! another hour has passed away.
Oh, time ! thy rapid current who can stay ?

And yet, how unimproved thy moments fly;
Mortals forget that they are born to die.

Death comes when least expected : who can tell
For whom may next be tolled the funeral knell?
The grey-hair'd sire, the blooming, and the brave,
The prince—the peasant—share one common
     grave.

We fondly gaze on those we loved to-day;
The morrow dawns, and where, oh ! where, are
     they ?
Lifeless and cold, their cherished forms are laid
In solemn silence, 'neath the grave's dark shade.

Religion—sacred treasure—but for thee,
The world a lonely wilderness would be;
Amid the darkest hour thou still art nigh,
To wipe the gushing tear from sorrow's eye.

Who would not give a thousand worlds to feel,
The calm serenity thou dost reveal ?
Oh ! sacred gem divine, to mortals given—
On earth our solace, and our guide to heaven.

But hush ! what sounds are stealing on my ear;
'Tis but the sighing of the winds I hear.
Oh ! there is music in each plaintive note—
How soft, yet mournful, o'er my soul they float.

How sweet, at such an hour, the parting sigh
To heave upon a mother's breast, and die ;
When the triumphant soul shall wing its flight,
To hail in heaven a morn of holier light.

'Twere sad to languish in a distant land,
Our pillow smoothed but by a stranger's hand ;
To pass the restless hours of night alone,
Without one heart congenial with our own.

No mother near, in soothing tones to speak ;
To bathe the aching head—the burning cheek.
Whence comes that shadowy form, with noise-
      less tread,
From the dark mansions of the lonely dead ?

Why trembles thus, my agitated frame ?
'Tis but the phantom of a fever'd brain ;
Nay see, it smiles benignant on me now,
A heavenly mildness sits upon that brow.

Speak, I conjure thee, habitant of bliss !
Say what has called thee to a world like this ?
Dost bring some message from yon starry sphere?
Then deign thine accents to a mortal ear.

" Frail child of earth, awake, delay no more,
Know thou the morn of life will soon be o'er :

Trust not the world, nor seek its smiles to gain,
False are its friendships, and its pleasures vain.

" Farewell! I'll still thy faithful guardian be,
While floats thy bark o'er life's tempestuous sea;
And when, oh! when the gathering storm shall
    cease,
Be thine the haven of eternal peace."

The vision speaks, then fading from my sight,
To heaven's celestial courts it wings its flight;
Night's dusky shadows quickly melt away,
And smiling nature hails the opening day.

NIAGARA.

A party from the Institution visited the Falls, in September, 1843 ; and the authoress, with several of her blind companions, ascended the Tower, and there traced the outline of their shape.

AWAKE, my muse ! thy wings expand !
  Oh, what sublimity is here !
Niagara's mighty thunders burst
  With awful grandeur on mine ear.
Niagara ! on thy brink I stand,
  And taste unutterable bliss ;
What pen, what language can pourtray
  A scene so wonderful as this ?
Father Divine !—we lift our hearts
  In humble gratitude to thee—
Who spread'st the azure vault above,
  Whose hand controls the boist'rous sea !
Thou bad'st the foaming cat'ract roll !
  Thou form'st the rainbow tints we see !
We gaze—we wonder and admire—
  Niagara !—we are lost in thee.

TO AN ABSENT DAUGHTER,

Oh, murmur not ! tho' deep the wound
  Thy Father's hand hath given ;
'Tis but to wean thy soul from earth,
  To purer joys in heaven.
What tho' our fondest hopes are crush'd,
  Our dearest ties are riven,
Tho' sundered here, we yet may meet
  To part no more—in heaven.
Dear, absent child ! thy parent's tears
  Flow for thy deep distress :
Their fondest prayers to heaven ascend,
  May God thy sorrows bless.
Then murmur not, tho' deep the wound
  Thy Father's hand hath given ;
Religion's pure and holy reign,
  Shall light thy soul to heaven.

TO A BOQUET.

Ye lovely gems of innocence !
  The objects of my constant care,
From each distracting thought I turn,
  To see you blooming fresh and fair.

What tho' the piercing wintry blast,
  Falls like a dirge upon my ear,
And the wild tempest loudly roars,—
  Sweet flowers, it cannot reach you here.

What do I see ?—your lovely forms
  Now languish!—must ye, then, decay ?
Ye pine for spring's refreshing showers,
  And for the sun's more genial ray.

Then, fare ye well !—your scentless leaves,
  I'll bathe with tears of fond regret;
I lov'd ye when you looked so fair—
  Wither'd and dead, I love you yet !

Thus, when some dear one, from our side,
  Is torn by death's cold hand away,
We mourn the cherish'd treasure gone,
  And weeping, kiss the lifeless clay.

O'er the bright joys forever crush'd,
  Will memory brood with fond regret;
We lov'd her when like us she smil'd,
  And tho' no more, we love her yet!

SONG,

"I'LL THINK OF THEE!"

(Music composed by F. J. C.)

I'LL think of thee, at that soft hour,
  When fade the parting hues of day,
And o'er each grove, and woodbine bow'r,
  The balmy gales of summer play.

When night around, her mantle throws,
  And stars illume the deep blue sea—
When wearied Nature seeks repose,
  Oh then—I'll dream—I'll dream of thee !

When from the east Aurora breaks,
  And night's dark shadows glide away;
When Nature from her slumber wakes,
  To hail with joy the op'ning day.

When sweetly bursting on mine ear,
  The tuneful warbler's note of glee,
I'll fondly fancy thou art near,
  To touch the "light guitar" for me.

On receiving a bouquet of roses

ON RECEIVING A BOUQUET OF ROSES,

FROM A FEMALE FRIEND.

THANKS, gentle one, for these sweet roses fair,
  Cull'd by thy hand, and rear'd so tenderly;
They are the objects of our fondest care—
  We kiss their blushing forms, and think of thee.

What, than the rose, more delicate appears?
  Yet, bitter thought, it blossoms to decay;
Like hopes in embryo dreams of other years,
  Or purest joys, that quickly pass away.

Dear friend, the rose of health is on thy cheek—
  Long, long unrivall'd, may it flourish there;
Those beaming eyes, in mildest language speak,
  The deep emotions of a heart sincere.

Oh! we could wish thine hours might glide away
  Calm and unruffl'd, as the moonlit stream;
That yon bright star—pure hope's celestial ray—
  Might with unsullied splendour, o'er thee beam.

SONG OF THE GREEK GIRL.

FAREWELL, guitar!—this faltering hand
  Will touch thy trembling chords no more!
Far from my lovely, native land,
  I languish on a distant shore;
    From Grecia's isle forever torn,
    A captive exile, now I mourn.

Farewell, guitar!—another hand
  Will wake thy trembling chords for me,
And in my own dear native land,
  Recal my favorite melody:
    The land where minstrels pour'd their lays,
    Where dwelt the bard of by-gone days.

Oh! might I find at last a grave
  In thee, my happy, happy isle!
The mournful cypress o'er me wave,
  And wild flowers sadly on me smile;
    There, bosom friends, and kindred dear,
    Would to my memory drop a tear.

ON THE DEATH OF AN AGED PARENT.

FAREWELL ! aged parent—farewell !
  Thy pilgrimage is o'er ;
The circle, by thy presence charm'd,
  Shall welcome thee no more.

Thy family, to thee so dear,
  Thy loss now deeply feel ;
The bitter grief that wrings their hearts,
  Their flowing tears reveal.

Oft has thy gen'rous hand reliev'd
  The orphan, and distress'd,
And they in humble gratitude,
  Thy name have often bless'd ;

And oh ! to thee, we fondly hope,
  A rich reward is given ;
That those who weep for thee on earth,
  Shall greet thee, yet, in heaven !

E*

THE SLEEPING INFANT OF A FRIEND.

YES, loved one! thou art sleeping;
  And on thy infant face,
A look of angel purity,
  Sweet innocent! I trace;
And while thy tranquil breathings
  Come softly on mine ear,
I know that seraphs guard thee,
  From yonder happy sphere.

Yes, lov'd one! thou art sleeping,
  I o'er the cradle bend,
And as I kiss thy spotless brow,
  My pray'rs to heaven ascend:
That He, who in his gracious arms
  On earth did infants take,
Will guard and keep thee, gentle flower,
  For thy dear parent's sake!

How tenderly they watch thee !
　Ah ! who their love can tell ?
And as thy infant mind expands,
　With joy their bosoms swell :
How oft thy laughing lips are press'd
　To thy fond mother's cheek,
And from her heart's pure font doth gush
　What words can never speak !

Sweet babe ! upon life's ocean,
　All peaceful may thou glide—
The idol of thy mother's heart,
　And thy fond father's pride !
And when by many a winter's frost,
　Their locks are silver'd o'er,
Oh ! may their first-born child be near,
　To cherish, and adore !

ON THE DEATH

OF THE FATHER OF A FELLOW PUPIL.

FATHER ! hast thou fled forever,
   From the friends who lov'd thee dear ?
Will thy soothing accents never
   Meet again thy children's ear ?

No, dear father, life is over ;
   Thou art freed from every pain ;
Death's cold hand has torn thee from us—
   We shall never meet again.

Ah ! methinks I see my mother,
   Bending o'er thy bed of death ;
On her cheek, now pale with anguish,
   Steals his last expiring breath.

By her stand my weeping sisters,
   Gazing on thy wasting frame,
While my brothers round thee hover,
   Mingling tears of grief and pain.

One deep struggle, and thy spirit
 Leaves its tenement of clay,
Borne, we trust, by guardian angels,
 To the brightest realms of day.

There no sigh shall heave thy bosom;
 There the pains of death are o'er;
There, dear father, may we meet thee,
 Never to be parted more.

TO A FRIEND AND FELLOW PUPIL,

WHO PROPOSED TO THROW AWAY THE FADED FLOWER OF A
FAVORITE PLANT.

CAST not this simple flower away !
I mark with sorrow its decay ;
But tho' its transient day be o'er,
Eliza, thou should'st love it more.

Though other flowers round it smile,
They'll blossom but a little while ;
Then, like my hyacinth decay :
Cast not that simple flower away.

The time may come, perchance ere long,
When she, whose light and joyous song
Thou oft hast heard, and in whose heart's
Affections thou dost share a part ;

May, like that wither'd flowret, fade,
And in the silent grave be laid.
With *her*, will all thy love decay ?—
Cast not that simple flower away !

TO A FRIEND AND FELLOW PUPIL. 59

Methinks I see the gathering tear
Fall from thine eyes, my sister dear;
Forgive, if I have caused thee pain—
I will not wound thy heart again.

Yet, by the love thou bear'st to me,
And my affection deep for thee,
Friend of my bosom, say, oh! say,
Thou wilt not cast that flower away!

ADDRESSED TO MISS D.,

THE MATRON WHO WAS ABOUT TO LEAVE THE INSTITUTION.

YES, thou art gazing with delight
  On those young flow'rets now;
Of them, I fain a wreath would twine,
  To place upon thy brow.
But, oh! methinks thou would prefer
  Wild nature's rural flowers,
That blossom by meand'ring streams,
  Or 'mid sequester'd bowers;
Then let me cull these lovely gems
  From some romantic spot,
The fairest, sweetest flower I bring,
  Shall be "forget me not!"—
"Forget me not!" alas! I soon
  To thee must bid farewell;
But need I say, within this heart
  Thy memory still shall dwell.
My heartfelt gratitude to thee
  These lips can never speak,
But thou may'st read it in the tear
  Warm gushing on my cheek.

In sickness thou hast o'er me watched—
 My every want supplied,
And nought I wish'd, that thou could'st grant,
 Was e'er to me denied.
I thank thee for each kind reproof,
 I have from thee received ;
But I acknowledge with regret,
 I thee too oft have grieved.
Forgive the faults of erring youth ;
 Believe my heart sincere ;
Its purest wishes are thine own,
 My friend, forever dear.
Oh ! would'st thou still with us remain,
 How happy we should be.
Vain wish—but, oh ! where'er thou art,
 May heaven still smile on thee.
Farewell ;—the dearest friends must part—
 The fondest ties be riven ;
But we may meet—oh ! blissful thought—
 To part no more, in heaven.

THE ORPHAN'S PRAYER.

INSCRIBED TO ANNA S.

Oh ! thou who sit'st enthroned in light,
  Above the starry frame,
To whom the supplicating voice
  Was never raised in vain,
Kind Father ! bend thy gracious ear,
Oh ! deign the orphan's prayer to hear.

Give me a calm, submissive heart,
  Thy chastening rod to bear ;
Let me not murmur at thy will,
  Nor yield me to despair.
The world has now no joys for me—
I dedicate my all to thee.

I have no tender mother now,
  My youthful steps to guide,
Oh ! I can ne'er forget the morn
  That gentle mother died.
She clasped me to her throbbing heart,
And softly whispered, we must part.

Weep not for me when I am gone,
  Nor heave one plaintive sigh,
I go to meet thy father dear,
  In realms beyond the sky.
Prepare, my child! to follow me
Where we no more shall severed be.

When nature by the tranquil breeze
  Of eve, is lulled to sleep,
Upon that mother's lonely grave
  I love to sit and weep,—
And while I kneel in sorrow there,
Kind Father! hear the orphan's prayer.

THE WISH.

I ASK; but not the glittering pomp
  Of wealth and pageantry;
Nor splendid dome; a rural cot,
  My domicil shall be.

'Tis not to mingle with the gay,
  The opulent, and proud;
'Tis not to court the flattering smile
  Of an admiring crowd.

I ask a heart—a faithful heart—
  Congenial with mine own,
Whose undivided love I share,
  Unenvied and alone.

A heart in sorrow's cheerless hour,
  To soften every care;
To taste with me the sweets of life,
  And all its ills to share.

Thus linked by friendship's golden chain,
  Ah! who more bless'd than we;
Unruffled as the pearly stream,
  Our halcyon days would be.

THE MANDAN CHIEF.

[The circumstance alluded to in the following lines, is that of the Mandan Chief, who, on the destruction of his tribe by the small pox, as the last survivor, rode to the prairies, where, after slaying his war-horse, destroyed himself.]

HE mounts his favorite steed of war,
  And o'er the prairie wild,
He speeds that fiery courser on—
  A lonely forest child.

His home is desolate and drear;
  His kindred, where are they?
That tribe, once powerful and brave,
  Disease hath swept away.

He yet survives; but what is life,
  When those we love are fled?
That Indian seeks a resting-place,
  Among the peaceful dead.

r*

And now he halts ; before him lies
  A vast expansive plain,
A moment, and that noble steed,
  By his own hand is slain.

Shade of my fathers ! he exclaims,
  I come with you to rest ;
He grasps the instrument of death,
  And plants it in his breast.

Fast streaming from the fatal wound,
  He sees the purple gore ;
'Tis done ! 'tis done ! he faintly cries,
  Then falls, to rise no more.

IMPROMPTU,

IN ANSWER TO THE QUESTION, "WILL YOU SEND FOR ME
WHEN YOU ARE ILL?"

THE promise I have made thee,
   Doubt not I will fulfil,
For I would have thee near me,
   My friend, when I am ill;
Yes, I would lay my aching head
   Upon thy faithful breast,
And while I felt its gentle throb,
   Would sweetly sink to rest.

Come throw thy arms about me,
   As thou hast oft before;
The song I lov'd so dearly,
   Oh! sing to me once more.
Yes, twine thine arms around me,
   And press thy cheek to mine;
The love that thus has warm'd me,
   Shall ever still be thine.

It was but yester-night I dream'd,
   In Eden's bower we strayed,
And sat, and talked of happiness,
   Beneath the olive shade.
There every tree, and plant, and flower,
   In all their beauty bloom'd,
And with their balmy fragrance,
   The evening air perfum'd.

Oh ! there is a fairer Eden,
   In yonder world above ;
There may we meet, no more to part,
   Friend of my fondest love.
There may thy voice in higher strains,
   Than it on earth can raise,
Be tuned with all the heavenly choir,
   To its Redeemer's praise.

LINES

Yes, she has fled, forever fled;
  That lovely flower has ceased to bloom;
Pale flowers, their silent perfume shed,
  On Henrietta's lonely tomb.

Her gentle voice in death is hushed
  Forever clos'd that sparkling eye,—
And fondest hopes, alas! are crush'd;
  Oh! 'tis a solemn thing to die.

For her do tender parents mourn;
  Their hearts are wrung with anguish deep;
To them she never can return—
  Yet, cease, dear parents, cease to weep.

Oh! trust, beyond this vale of tears,
  Her soul has gone to heaven's bright shore;
Sweet thought;—a few more fleeting years
  And you shall meet to part no more.

Sisters, for her, whom all did love,
　Oh! wake not sorrow's plaintive strain,
Methinks from yonder world above,
　She whispers " we shall meet again."

You stood around her dying bed ;
　You kiss'd her cold and lifeless clay ;
You laid her with the silent dead ;
　Yet, two, alas! were far away.

Oh! thou who hear'st the mourner's cry—
　Thou who did'st weep o'er Lazarus dead—
Oh! sweetly calm each heaving sigh,
　And wipe the bitter tears they shed.

Watch o'er them, Lord, with tender care,
　While from their native land they roam,
And spare, oh! heavenly guardian, spare,
　And bring them safely to their home.

EASTER SUNDAY.

HAIL, sacred morn ! when from the tomb
   The Son of God arose,
" Captivity he captive led,"
   And triumph'd o'er his foes.

Rejoice ! oh, holy church, rejoice !
   Awake thy noblest strain,
Put off thy weeds of mourning now,
   The Saviour lives again.

Oh ! let thy loud hosannahs reach
   The portals of the sky,
While angels tune their gentle harps
   And heav'nly choirs reply.

" Glory to God ! he ever lives
   To plead our cause above,
He,—he is worthy to receive
   All honor, power, and love.

" Hail, mighty king ! we at thy feet
   Our grateful homage pay,
Accept the humble sacrifice,
   And wash our sins away.

" Then at the resurrection morn,
   When the last trump shall sound,
May we awake to life anew,
   And with thy saints be found."

ON THE DEATH OF A CHILD.

SLEEP on, thou lovely one ! sleep on,
  While o'er thy lonely grave,
The mournful breeze of evening sighs,
  And the pale flowrets wave.

Sweet bud ! too soon death's icy hand
  Hath borne thee to the tomb,
But thou in purer loveliness,
  In Paradise shall bloom.

Oh ! there was one that o'er thee knelt,
  And wept from thee to part,
Who gazed upon thy lifeless form,
  With almost bursting heart.

She breathed a kiss upon those lips,
  That still in death were fair,
She spoke not ; language could not paint,
  That mother's deep despair.

G

And was there none to sooth her grief,
   And wipe the bitter tear,
That from her swollen eyelids burst ?
   Ah ! yes, thy father dear.

The partner of her early love,
   With her beside thee knelt,
He strove to hide the bitter grief
   His stricken bosom felt.

" Weep not," he said, in faltering tones,
   " Our darling one has fled,
But he who gave, has borne her hence ;
   Then weep not for the dead."

" Soon from this transitory world,
   Shall our glad spirits soar,
To meet in heaven our darling child,
   Where parting is no more."

THE NEGLECTED CHILD.

HER home was by the mountain side,
  Where verdure gaily smil'd;
No ray illum'd the sightless eyes,
  Of the neglected child.

She heard the breezes murmur by,
  And the streamlet rush along;
And wildly on her ear, would break,
  Her native Alpine song.

No fond emotions of delight,
  Her lonely hours beguil'd;
None wip'd the tear-drop from the cheek,
  Of that neglected child.

Alas! no bosom friend was near,
  Her rising grief to quell;
For in a far, far distant land,
  Did her fond parents dwell.

She felt the genial sunny beam,
   That o'er her gently smil'd,
But ah! no ray illum'd the path,
   Of the neglected child.

Thus months and years roll'd cheerless on,
   In pensiveness and grief;
When heaven, all bounteous and kind,
   Gave her sad heart relief.

Parental love she felt once more—
   A father on her smiled—
And warmly to his heart he press'd,
   The long neglected child.

But joys—far sweeter joys than these—
   The sightless girl did feel;
And down her cheek, the heartfelt tear
   Of gratitude did steal.

Then education, to her mind,
   Its blessings did impart;
A ray of gladness brightly shone,
   In that young docile heart.

Her fingers trace the sacred page,
   By inspiration given;
Her guide through life's lone wilderness,—
   The chart that points to heaven.

Forever be those joys her own,
   That long have on her smil'd ;
Dear to my heart shall be the name,
   Of the neglected child.

"JESUS WEPT."

JOHN xi. 35.

HE wept! the son of God—the Saviour wept!—
When at the lowly grave where Laz'rus slept;—
He wept—for oh! his human nature felt
Their grief, who at his feet in sorrow knelt.
He wipes the tear from sorrow's weeping eye—
He calms the troubled breast, the heaving sigh;
And tho' his rod we feel, in love 't is giv'n,—
'Tis but to raise our hearts from earth to heav'n.
He for our sins did die—oh! wondrous love!
He, with his Father pleads our cause above:
The contrite spirit, He will not disdain—
The soul that seeks him, shall not seek in vain.
Tho' tempests rise, if we on him are staid,
He'll whisper—I am here—" be not afraid."
Tho' earthly friends forsake, He still is nigh,
To guard his children with a watchful eye.

ERIN.

Oh! Erin, lovely isle! for thee
  My tears of heartfelt pity flow;
Wilt still a monarch's vassal be?
  The voice of Freedom answers, no!

Too long, oppression's galling chain,
  Thou injur'd Isle, thy sons have worn!
Crush'd, and despis'd, their rights profaned;
  Oh, say, shall wrongs like these be borne?

Just indignation fires my breast,
  The child of blood-bought liberty;
I cannot see that land oppress'd,
  Though not mine own, but dear to me.

Why should not Freedom's banner wave,
  O'er Erin's isle its noble crest?
Is there a heart, I ask, more brave,
  Than beats within an Irish breast?

Go thou—her cool, soft breeze, inhale—
　　Whose mind stern prejudice doth close ;
Beneath her lofty shades regale,
　　Or by her noble streams repose.

Would'st thou on splendour feast thine eyes ?
　　Thou many a stately dome may'st see ;
If rural scenes thou dearer prize,
　　There Nature opes her store for thee—

Wreathe for thy brow a chaplet fair—
　　There bloom rich flowers of every hue,
The daisy, and the primrose rare,
　　And Erin's pride, the *shamrock*, too.

Nay, scorn it not ! the shamrock green,
　　The shamrock Erin loves so dear ;—
While tracing each enchanting scene,
　　To Ireland's misery give a tear.

Hark ! heard'st thou not that stifled sigh,
　　That from her children doth proceed ?
Senseless and cold thy heart must be,
　　If for their wrongs it would not bleed !

If thine Columbia's happy land,
　　Where Liberty's bright star doth smile,
When on its peaceful shores thou stand,
　　Think of the lovely Emerald Isle.

And when before thy Father's throne,
  Thou supplicate his gracious smile—
Unseen, save by his eye alone,
  Forget not then, the Emerald Isle.

"MY NATIVE LAND, GOOD NIGHT!"

Adieu! adieu! my native land—
  I leave thy happy shore;
Oh! bitter thought! perhaps to view
  Thy lovely scenes no more.

My gallant bark, her sails unfurl,
  The stars are beaming bright;
Bird-like, she floats upon the wave,
  " My native land, good night!"

The rugged hills, the mountain wild,
  Where once I lov'd to stray,
While birds, their little notes of glee,
  Caroll'd from spray to spray.

Alas! these rural scenes are fast
  Receding from my sight;
One lingering look on thee I cast,
  " My native land, good night!"

The crystal brook, that gently glides
  Beside my peaceful cot,
Fresh flow'rs that breathe their sweet perfume
  Around that lovely spot.

The mighty Hudson, on whose breast
  I've gazed with fond delight—
All, all are fading from my view,
  " My native land, good night !"

THE EMIGRANT.

He drop't a tear,—disease had laid
  That aged pilgrim low;
He drop't a tear,—for memory touch'd
  A chord, that bade it flow.

His hands were folded on his breast,
  He knew he soon must die;
But 'twas not the approach of death,
  That dimm'd with tears his eye.

" Farewell! dear native land, farewell!"
  In broken tones he said;
" Alas! my ashes must repose,
  Where strangers' feet will tread!

" My wife—my ever faithful wife,—
  One parting word to thee;
Oh, let me clasp thy hand once more,
  Yet weep not thus for me!

" The widow's God will still be thine,
  Thy comforter, and guide;"

And to the church-yard he was borne,
  With slow and solemn tread ;
They laid his pale and lifeless form
  Among the silent dead.

The grave was closed—they left the spot—
  But one still linger'd there,
Whose agonizing look bespoke,
  Her bosom's deep despair.

She sought her home—that home, alas !
  Was desolate and drear ;—
She trod the threshold, but no voice
  Of welcome, met her ear.

She was a stranger, and alone ;
  All kindred ties were riven ;
And now, with those she lov'd so dear,
  Her spirit blends in heaven.

AN ADDRESS

TO THE REV. DR. HEWITT, OF BRIDGEPORT, CONN.

SERVANT of God! His gracious eye
   Beholds thee with delight!
The flock which to thy trust he gives,
   Is precious in his sight.

Press on! ambassador from Christ!
   Thou a reward shall reap;
For souls, with gospel truths impress'd,
   Shall wake from error's sleep.

Be not disheartened, though thy words
   May seem to flow in vain;
The Lord will soon his word revive,
   And souls be born again.

Thou to thy faithful flock art dear,
   Their pastor, and their friend,
And often at the mercy seat,
   Your supplications blend.

Soon will thy pilgrimage be o'er,
   Thy work on earth be done ;
And thou the welcome plaudit hear,
   " Servant of God ! well done !"

AN EPITHILAMIUM

ON MEETING A FRIEND, AFTER HER MARRIAGE.

WE meet again—we meet again—
  Thou art as lovely now,
As when those auburn tresses last
  I parted from thy brow.

Time has not chang'd thee—no, thine eye
  Still dances with delight—
The same fond smile is on thy lip,
  Thy bosom still is light.

We meet again, but who is he,
  That lingers at thy side,
That holds thy trembling hand in his,
  And on thee looks with pride ?

Thy partner ?—yes ! the bridal wreath,
  Is on thy brow so fair ;
He to the altar thee has led—
  Oh, happy, happy pair !

And may the gentle star of peace,
  Your guardian ever be ;
Your little bark serenely glide,
  · O'er an unruffled sea.

We meet again—we meet again—
  Thou art as lovely now,
As when those auburn tresses last
  I parted from thy brow.

"SPEED ME TO MY HOME."

Oh ! bear me to that blissful clime,
   My bosom holds so dear,
And let the murmur of its stream,
   Fall sweetly on my ear.

I love not India's sultry land—
   I wish no more to roam,—
Unfurl thy snowy sails, my bark !
   And speed me to my home.

O'er bonny Scotland's highland hills,
   At twilight hour I've stray'd,
While on the bosom of the Clyde
   The silver moonbeams play'd.

But, on the Hudson's sunny banks,
   I long once more to roam ;
Unfurl thy snowy sails, my bark !
   And speed me to my home.

I've sat beneath the rural shade,
  Of England's rosy bowers,
I've heard the music of her birds,
  And cull'd her fairest flowers.

But to Columbia, dearer land,
  My fancy loves to roam ;
Unfurl thy snowy sails, my bark !
  And speed me to my home.

THE GUITAR.

ON PRESENTING TO A FRIEND AND FELLOW PUPIL,

ANNA S., HER GUITAR.*

Oh ! Anna dear, my light guitar,
  I would bequeath to thee ;
I cannot bear its music now,
  It hath no charms for me.
Yes, take it—keep it for my sake,
I may no more its numbers wake.

But thou its dulcet chords wilt sweep,
  At twilight's dewy hour,
And thou wilt wake my favorite lay,
  In thine own rosy bower.
Then while thy heart is full of grief,
Oh, Anna ! wilt thou think of me ?

* The instrument was laid aside by the advice of her
physician.

Think of those happy, happy hours ;
   We have together pass'd,
The cherished hopes of other years,
   Too pure, too bright to last.
On thy fond bosom I have wept,
When all around us gently slept.

The rose of health hath fled my cheek,
   And something to my heart,
Is sadly whispering, I ere long
   With thee, dear friend, must part ;
Thine was to me a sister's love,
That flame shall light our souls above.

Oh, God ! protect this orphan one,
   With thy parental care ;
And leave her not the cruel storms,
   Of this bleak world to bear ;
But may affection's hallow'd smile,
Her pilgrimage on earth beguile.

TO A SPIRIT.

COME on the breeze at the twilight hour,
When I muse alone in my leaf-clad bower,
There let thy gentle voice be heard,
Like the carol sweet of some favorite bird,
Breathe o'er the chords of my slumbering lute,
Tones that, alas ! have long been mute.

Come, on the balmy breath of night,
When the pale moon is spreading her silv'ry light,
O'er the sylvan grove and the chrystal deep,
And nature is lock'd in her dreamy sleep ;
Leave the pure mansions of bliss awhile—
Come, on thy youth's companion smile.

Come, when the cheerful voice of spring,
Gaily through woodland and grove doth ring ;
Come, when the cuckoo's welcome note,
Sweetly and clear on the breeze doth float,
Wandering alone 'mid the silent glen,
Hover, oh ! hover, around me then.

Come, when the tear of sorrow flows ;
Thou, and thou only, could'st sooth my woes;
Come, when my cheek is pale with care,
Or the hectic flush is lurking there ;
Oh! how I sigh for thy starry home,
Never, oh ! never, again to roam.

IMPROMPTU.

LINES ADDRESSED TO GEN. COUNT BERTRAND, ON VISIT-
ING THE INSTITUTION, NOV. 1843.

WELCOME, thou illustrious General!
To Columbia's lovely shore—
Welcome, thou illustrious General!
Well may France thy name adore.

On her throne, in splendor seated,
Did the brave Napoleon reign;
Flattering courtiers gathered round him,
Distant nations sang his fame.

But, alas! o'er fallen greatness,
Was that monarch doomed to mourn,
And an exile from his country,
To St. Helen's Isle was borne.

When by those he lov'd deserted,
Thine was still a faithful heart;
Thou wert proud to share the exile
Of the hapless Bonaparte.

Like an angel, whispering comfort,
  Still in sickness thou wert nigh ;
And when life's last scenes were over,
  Tears of anguish dimmed thine eye.

He has gone ! yes, gone forever,
  But around thy generous heart,
Ties that only death can sever,
  Twine the name of Bonaparte.

Welcome, then, illustrious General !
  We, a sightless band exclaim ;
Laurels of immortal honor,
  Wreath their garlands o'er thy name.

Welcome, thou, illustrious General !
  We rejoice to meet thee here ;
We, alas ! cannot behold thee,
  But thy voice may glad our ear.

When thou o'er the deep art sailing,
  Where the angry tempests roar,
We implore our God to bear thee
  Safely to thy native shore.

I

REQUIEM ON GENERAL BERTRAND,

ON HEARING OF HIS DECEASE.

HARK! o'er yonder pathless ocean,
  Comes a voice of bitter woe;
France in sorrow's weeds is shrouded—
  Death hath laid her hero low.

List ye, to the mournful tidings,
  Sons of fair Columbia's shore!
Drop, oh! drop, one tear of pity,
  Marshal Bertrand is no more.

He, whom recently ye welcomed
  With emotions of delight,
To this lovely land; where freedom
  Waves aloft its banner bright;—

He who deeply felt your kindness,
  And who blest our happy shore,
In the silent grave is sleeping;
  Marshal Bertrand is no more.

Scarcely had his friends receiv'd him
  To his native land again;
Scarcely heard their joyous greeting,
  Ere to him death's summons came.

Fare thee well, illustrious General!
  Now thy pilgrimage is o'er,—
Far the mournful news is echoed,
  Marshal Bertrand is no more.

On the gentle breeze of evening,
  Comes his requiem, soft and low,—
Keen, oh, France! must be thine anguish,
  But 'tis meet thy tears should flow.

He who for thy fallen monarch,
  Exiled from his native shore,
Tore himself from home and country,
  Marshal Bertrand is no more.

'Till Napoleon's latest moments,
  Bertrand was his constant friend,
With unwearied care beguiling
  Grief that only death must end.

Faint and yet more faint the struggle;
  Bertrand knelt beside his bed,
On his hand, his head reclining,
  Wept in silence o'er the dead.

Years rolled on, and from St. Helen's,
  Back to France, his corpse they bore,—
By whose side will rest his ashes—
  Marshal Bertrand now no more.

May we hope that tranquil spirit,
  Doth in heaven's bright mansions dwell;
Once again, in faltering accents,
  Marshal Bertrand! fare thee well.

ON THE DEPARTURE OF A TEACHER.

Kind teacher, must we part with thee ?
  Wilt thou no longer with us dwell?
Ah, no—it must not, cannot be,
  Thou wilt not breathe the sad farewell.

Oh ! who will now thy place supply ?
  Who will instruction now impart ?
The tear-drop steals from every eye,
  And sorrow bursts from every heart.

Yet memory still shall cling to thee,
  On happier days our thoughts shall dwell;
But, oh ! it must not, cannot be,
  Thou wilt not breathe the sad farewell.

Yet, if thou must from us remove,
  Oh ! let us willingly submit;
Accept thy pupils' grateful love,
  Thy kindness they will ne'er forget.

May Hope's bright beams still smile on thee,
  And pleasure with thee ever dwell;
But, no ! it must not, cannot be—
  Thou wilt not breathe the sad farewell.

LINES TO A FAVORITE WILLOW.

FAREWELL, old tree ! beneath whose shade,
  I lov'd at twilight hour to sit :
Thee to the ground the axe hath laid,
  I view thee now with fond regret.

Here, with my young companions gay,
  I've sported oft in by-gone days,—
Here at the closing hour of day,
  I've heard soft music's thrilling lays.

When Venus, evening's fav'rite star,
  Shone forth from yonder clear blue sky,
Here have I tuned my light guitar,
  To some romantic melody.

But thou art gone, forever gone !
  These happy days, alas ! are o'er,
The light guitar, the joyous song,
  Will echo from thy shade no more.

Could tears the woodman's axe have stay'd,
  I would have freely wept for thee ;
Oh ! how I sigh for thy dear shade,
  Sacred to memory and me.

TO A STAR.

Thou radiant orb, whose twinkling beams,
Smile o'er the distant mountain streams,
I've watched thee oft, with eager eye,
As in the calm, cerulean sky,
Thou dost a constant vigil keep,
O'er lovely nature's peaceful sleep.

What art thou? may I read in thee,
Aught of my future destiny?
Can'st thou some hidden joy reveal,
Or pang, this bosom yet must feel?
Can'st thou recall to me the past
Departed hopes, too bright to last!

By whom to thee was radiance given?
Who guides thee through the pathless heaven?
Art thou a sun, whose golden ray,
Doth light to other worlds convey;
Worlds where the ever verdant flowers,
Bloom in their bright Elysian bowers?

And sweeter than Apollo's lyre,
The music of the ærial choir ;—
Love not the muses there to dwell,—
Their notes in magic strains to swell?
Fain would I soar, mild orb ! to thee,
But thou art veiled in mystery.

FAREWELL TO THE SUMMER FLOWER.

Farewell ! farewell, to the summer flowers !
They are faded and gone from their greenwood
    bowers ;
One drooping lily alone I see,
And the lovely gem I have culled for thee.

'Twill wither ere long, and thy fondest care,
Will be lavished in vain on that flowret fair ;
'Tis an emblem of childhood's hours long past,
Bright hours we could wish might forever last.

'Tis evening now, and the sun's last gleam,
Is bidding adieu to the mountain stream ;
I'm sweeping my harp's wild notes to thee—
Then list to thy favorite melody.

Mournful breezes around me sigh,
And the starry train from the deep blue sky,
Serenely smile o'er the rippling sea—
Then list to thy favorite melody.

ON THE DEPARTURE OF A PUPIL

FROM THE INSTITUTE.

DEAR brother, farewell! since the word must be
    spoken,
And thou from our circle far distant must dwell;
Oh! ne'er shall the tie that unites us be broken—
May heaven protect thee, dear brother, farewell!

Here long have we dwelt, and the pure stream
    of gladness,
Around us hath flowed, like a rill thro' the dell,
All waveless and calm—but a billow of sadness,
Now ruffles its waters—dear brother, farewell!

Thou leav'st us, but friends in transport will
    meet thee—
Thou goest to the home of thy childhood to dwell;
And oh! when maternal affection doth greet thee,
Forget not the friends who now bid thee farewell!

THE GRECIAN WAR SONG.

AWAKE ! awake, my tuneful lyre !
  The notes of minstrelsy ;
I'll sing to thee, my native land,
  A song of liberty !

The Persian band are at our gates,
  Their glitt'ring arms I see—
They chant our death-song in our ears,
  But Greece shall yet be free !

On ! Grecian warriors, to the field !
  Your bleeding country save ;
On ! on ! the victory achieve !
  Or share the hero's grave.

They wave the crimson sword on high—
  Haste—ere they strike the blow !
Your swords, proud Grecians, to the earth,
  Shall crush the faithless foe.

CHILDHOOD.

Come back, oh! come back, to this bosom once
    more,
  Ye days of my childhood—long, long pass'd
    away—
To the warblers that caroll'd their melodies o'er,
  I listened, as buoyant and happy as they;
Bright garlands I twined, of the wild fragrant
    flowers,
As I basked in the sunbeams that smiled in the
    bowers.

Oh, where is the oak that majestic'ly stood,
  And braved the wild tempest that swept o'er
    its head!
Oh, where is my cottage, beside the greenwood?
  'Tis echo, all mournful, replies, they are fled:
They are fled, and a stranger, forgotten, I roam;
Farewell to my kindred! my dear native home!

Come back, oh! come back, to this desolate heart,
  My youthful companions, to friendship sincere;
Ah! why was I doomed, from those loved ones
    to part—
  To moisten their graves with affection's sad tear?
They are gone, and a stranger, unpitied, I roam,
Farewell to my kindred! my long-cherish'd home.

ODE ON THE FOURTH OF JULY.

Awake ! ye brave sons of Columbia, awake !
See the morn of your freedom resplendently
    break ;
A shout o'er the East and the West doth resound,
And the North and the South sweetly echo the
    sound.

Columbia ! Columbia ! transported arise ;
Let thy altars of freedom be rear'd to the skies;
United forever our nation shall be ;
Hurrah for Columbia, the land of the free !

Oh ! Washington, Warren, Montgomery, ye
    brave,
Smile, smile, o'er the country you struggled to
    save :
Here liberty's tree unmolested still grows,
And we 'neath its shadowy branches repose.

No more shall the war-cry be heard on thy shore,
Thrice happy Columbia, thy struggles are o'er,—
United for ever our nation shall be—
Hurrah for Columbia, the land of the free !

K

LINES ADDRESSED TO C. B. ESQ.,

ON NEW YEAR'S DAY, 1842.

KIND friend—these effusions, I tender to you,
  Whose kindness has taught me your name to
  ·   revere ;
May blessings descend, like the soft evening dew,
  And crown the return of this " happy New
  Year."

As the gondola glides o'er the calm summer sea,
  'Mid the wild *canzonet* of the gay gondolier,
Oh ! thus may life's moments, unruffled still be—
  And each return bring you a " happy New
  Year."

My heart's kindest wishes, on you I bestow,
  For zeal, still unwearied and friendship sin-
  cere ;
And still from my bosom these accents shall flow,
  I "wish you" full many a "happy New Year."

"MY PRAIRIE HOME."

ADDRESSED TO MR. B. M.

OH! I have dwelt in sunny isles,
   Far, far, beyond the sparkling deep,
Where nature ever verdant smiles,
   'Mid skies that never, never weep;
And I have plucked each fragrant flower,
Luxuriant from its native bower.

There birds with gaudy plumes arrayed,
   Carol their plaintive songs at night,
And through the deep accacian shade,
   The crescent moon unveils her light;
As o'er each magic scene I'd roam,
I have sighed for thee, " my prairie home."

Speed lightly on, my gallant bark!
   Unfurl once more thy snowy sails—
Speed lightly on, o'er waters dark;
   Now gently blow the spicy gales,—
O'er distant lands no more I'll roam,
But haste to thee, " my prairie home."

Earth has no dearer spots for me,
  Than thy expansive meadows are,
The peaceful dwellings of the free;
  The deer is wildly bounding there;
And on the breeze in joyous notes,
The pioneer's sweet chorus floats.

GENEVA.

COMPOSED WHILE ON A VISIT TO THAT PLACE, IN 1843.

GENEVA ! thou spot ever dear to my heart,
Our State's lovely Eden, sweet village, thou art;
Thy groves of rich verdure, delighted I tread,
While flow'rets around me their soft perfume
  shed.

Before me thy lake, all majestic and clear,
Whose murmurs, like music, now float on my ear,
Reflects, like a mirror, the sun's golden beam,—
On its calm, silvery breast, not a ripple is seen.

Yet, while 'neath the shade of thy green woods I
  stray,
I weep, for thy beauties ere long will decay ;
The keen breath of autumn will sweep o'er thy
  lawn,
And hush'd be the notes of the wild warbler's song.

Yet, not for thy beauties alone art thou dear,
Geneva ! the friends warmly cherished are here,
Whose mem'ries enshrined in our bosoms remain,
Whose kindness our grateful emotions doth claim.

   K*

Farewell, lovely spot ! ever dear to this heart,
From thy scenes so enchanting, alas ! I must part.
Dear friends, in this bosom your kindness shall
    dwell,
May blessings attend you, ye lov'd ones—fare-
    well !

SOLITUDE.

Oh! rural life, I sigh for thee,
How dear thy rustic haunts to me;
I, in some lonely spot would dwell,
And bid the busy world farewell.

I seek not its applause to gain;
Its flattering words are false and vain;
Its smiles are like the summer showers;
Its friendships die like withered flowers.

Oh! that some humble cot were mine,
Where peace, a fadeless wreath might twine,
And envy, strife, and anxious care,
Might never, never, reach me there.—

Where no discordant notes should ring,
But sweetest rapture tune each string,
And friendship's pure and hallowed smile
Fondly each fleeting hour beguile.

ON THE DEATH OF GENERAL HARRISON,

APRIL, 1841.

HE is gone ! in death's cold arms he sleeps,
  Our President—our hero brave,
While fair Columbia o'er him weeps,
  And chants the requiem o'er his grave ;
Her sanguine hopes are blighted now,
And weeds of sorrow veil her brow.

Ah ! Indiana, where is he,
  Who once thy sons to battle led ?
The red man quailed beneath his eye,
  And from his camp disheartened fled ;
With steady hand he bent his bow,
And laid the warlike savage low.

The forests with his praises rung,
  His fame was echo'd far and wide,—
With loud hurrah, his name was sung,
  Columbia's hero, and her pride.
The tuneful harp is now unstrung,
And on the drooping willow hung,

Him for our President we chose,
   To execute the nation's laws;
While from each gladdened heart arose
   Loud acclamations of applause;
Scarce had his arduous work begun,
When set fair freedom's favorite son.

Within the dark and lonely cell,
   No anxious cares shall reach him more;
Illustrious patriot, fare thee well!
   Thy earthly pilgrimage is o'er;
With Washington, our father, friend,
Thy fame undying, now we blend.

THE LAMENT OF MRS. HARRISON.

My heart-strings are breaking, oh! sad is my lay,
　My hero, my bosom companion, is fled ;
Oh, death ! why so soon did'st thou tear him
　　away
　From his home, and his country, to sleep with
　　the dead ?

No more shall he bleed in America's cause,
　Or lead to the battle the dauntless and brave,
Though hush'd are the shouts of a nation's
　　applause,
　The laurels of victory bloom o'er his grave.

A mantle of gloom shrouds the Capitol now,
　Columbia, her President's loss doth deplore ;
A shade of despondency veils every brow,
　And the sound of rejoicing is echo'd no more.

Oh! could I have watch'd the last moments of life,
    And from those dear lips, caught the parting
      farewell;
But far from his home, his children, and wife,
    His last sigh was breath'd,—his last accents fell.

No more shall his soothings my sorrow beguile,
    Then what are earth's varied enjoyments to
      me?
The summons of death I could meet with a smile,
    My soul like a captive doth sigh to be free.

LINES

Written on hearing of the death of the Hon. H. S. Legare, of South Carolina, late Secretary of State, at Boston, while on a tour with the President of the U. S., June, 1843.

FAREWELL!—esteemed, departed one—farewell!
Deep, solemn tones, have pealed their funeral
    knell!
Thou to the grave art gone—sweet be thy rest,
For angels guard the relics of the blest.

Hark! hark! thy requiem floats upon the ear,
So deeply sad!—we pause—we weep to hear.
Ye patriot sons, of fair Columbia's shore,
A brilliant star has set, to rise no more.

Weep, oh, Columbia! o'er his lonely grave,
There let the cypress, sorrow's emblem, wave;
The mournful breezes sigh, wild flowret's bloom,
And breathe their fragrance o'er his hallowed
    tomb.

Far from his home, he closed his bright career:
His dying words were of his sister dear,—
His only relative !   Oh, gracious heaven !
Her heart will break;—its last fond tie is riven.

Oh, God ! convulsive throbs her bosom now ;
Her tresses fall neglected on her brow ;
Her streaming eyes, uplifted, turn to thee,
Friend of the orphan ! still her guardian be.

Legare !— thy name, thy country will revere,
Thou wast her pride—she smiled to call thee
          dear ;
But, thou art gone to join that patriot band,
Whose spirits hover o'er this happy land.

Illustrious statesman !—orator—farewell !
Our quivering lips in mournful accents swell,—
While we thy loss, disconsolate, deplore,
Hope whispers, we may meet to part no more.

THE SISTER'S LAMENT.

Oh ! lightly press yon clay cold sod,
   Where doth the mournful cypress wave ;
Oh ! lightly press yon clay cold sod,—
   It wraps an only brother's grave.

Lone is my heart, its idol fled ;
   I call him, but, alas ! in vain,—
He's number'd with the mighty dead—
   We ne'er shall meet on earth again.

Oh ! could I for a moment felt,
   Upon my cheek his parting breath,
Oh ! could I at his bedside knelt,
   And kiss'd those lips, tho' closed in death.

'Twould sooth the grief, that wrings my heart,
   To think he on my bosom died ;
But, stranger hands perform'd the part,
   That was, alas ! to me denied.

Brother! thy voice I nowhere hear,
   No more thy gentle smile I see,—
But thy pure spirit hovers near,
   And will thy sister's guardian be.

And, oh! when life's last scenes are o'er,
   May my glad soul, on wings of love,
Be wafted to yon heavenly shore,
   Where all is happiness above.

There may I meet thee, brother dear!
   And never, never part again;
Where wip'd away, is every tear—
   Where comes not sorrow's plaintive strain.

THEY ARE GONE.

They are gone! those bright and blissful hours,
When the soft wind laugh'd, 'mid the green-
    wood bowers,
And the night-bird caroled its plaintive lay,
As faded the crimson tints of day.

And the dew-drop came, at the twilight close,
To sleep on the breast of the mountain rose;
They are gone! those blissful hours are passed,
And a snowy garb on the earth is cast.

And, oh! when the friends we lov'd are fled,
To the cold, cold mansions of the dead;
Like the fragile flower, may we cease to bloom,
And sleep with them in the peaceful tomb.

TO LAKE ERIE.

On Erie's banks, when morn's bright green,
  Dispels the shades of night,
And sprinkles o'er the dewy lawn,
  Her rosy tints of light.

I stood ; with ecstacy I gazed
  Upon its glassy breast—
The winds were hush'd, its billows slept
  Calm as an infant's rest.

Oh ! I could dwell, forever dwell
  'Mid such a scene as this,
Could o'er yon lake's fair bosom glide,
  Nor dream of aught but bliss.

Yet, no ; it must not, cannot be,
  I may not linger here,
Then, Erie, lovely lake ! farewell
  I leave thee with a tear.

L*

TO A FAVORITE PLANT.

Farewell, lovely flow'ret ! thy delicate form
Is crushed by the breath of the bleak winter storm ;
Too rudely, alas ! hath it swept o'er thy head,
Thy leaves once so fragrant, lie withered and dead.

I have seen thee when beauty's pure smile was
      thine own ;
I sigh'd to behold thee thus languish alone ;
Bright Phœbus in vain doth his beams o'er thee
      shed,
Thy leaves once so fragrant, lie withered and dead.

No more will the dew-drop be rock'd on thy
      breast,
Sweetly lull'd by the soft breathing zephyr to rest ;
But the tear of affection shall moisten thy bed,
Tho' thy leaves once so fragrant lie withered and
      dead.

A ROSE.

I saw at e'en a blushing rose,
   'Twas delicate and fair,
The dew-drop on its bosom slept;
   Its fragrance filled the air.

I gazed upon its fragile form,
   While zephyrs round it blew,
And longed to pluck it from the bush,
   On which it fondly grew.

I turned to watch a placid stream,
   That murmured at my side,
As through a deep and flowery vale
   It rapidly did glide.

Unclouded was the deep blue sky,
   Night's silvery queen rose bright,
And o'er the bosom of that stream,
   She poured her gentle light.

I turned again to view my rose,
　　But it no more was gay,
A canker worm was at its root,
　　And threatened its decay.

Thus, like the rose, the lovely youth,
　　In innocence may bloom,
And soon, by death's resistless hand,
　　Is hurried to the tomb.

THE TEAR.

WHEN tossed on the deep, where the ocean
    waves foam,
  And the surge dashes wild on the ear,
How sweet the reflection that lov'd ones at home
    Will shed o'er our absence a tear.

When we of the sunshine of hope are bereft,
  And our path is all lonely and drear;
When as oft not a ray to console us is left,
  There's a solace in sympathy's tear.

And when on the ear some old melody breaks,
  That in youth we delighted to hear,
A thousand fond scenes in our bosom awakes
  While bursts from our eye the sad tear.

When the last rays of evening are faded and gone,
  And the moon her pale lustre discloses,
When hush'd are the notes of the nightingale's
    song,
  And nature in silence reposes,—

How sweet to revisit the grave of a friend,
  When our sighs none but heaven can hear;
To kiss the cold stone, as in sadness we bend,
  And moisten her name with a tear.

REFLECTIONS AFTER A DRIVE.

My swelling heart is bursting with delight,
  Again I feel the balmy breath of spring;
The genial sun is beautiful and bright;
  I hear the merry warblers sweetly sing.

On rolls the vehicle—away! away!
  Through many a wild, romantic spot we glide,
Here waking flowers their opening buds display;
  There streamlets murmur by the green hill
    side.

Oh! when from cage released, the captive bird
  Spreads her light wings, and gaily soars in air;
Whose carol, 'mid sequester'd groves is heard,
  My buoyant spirit may with her compare.

No threatening clouds o'ercast my sunny sky;
  No dark, foreboding thoughts my peace alloy;
The rapid moments float unheeded by,
  Mine is indeed a lot of purest joy.

'Tis evening's tranquil hour of peaceful rest,
   And silent now each sportive note of mirth,
While mellow light out from the crimson west,
   Looks forth, all lovely, o'er the sleeping earth.

Tho' all alone, I'm not less happy now,
   Than when I mingled with the busy throng,
There comes a pleasing sadness o'er my brow,
   My muse with pensive thoughts inspires my
      song.

How soon our brightest moments pass away,
   And but the memory of their scenes is left;
Scarcely we hail the dawn of pleasure's ray,
   Ere we, alas! are of that ray bereft.

The rapid vehicle, no more I see,
   Its rolling sound upon mine ear hath died,—
Yet on the tablet of my heart, shall be
   Engraved the memory of that happy ride.

LINES,

INSCRIBED TO PROFESSOR R., INSTRUCTOR IN MUSIC AT
THE INSTITUTION.

Oh, Germany! thrice happy land,
  Where youth's gay morning passed away,
Though on a distant shore I stand,
  To thee my thoughts still love to stray;
And memory, on thy scenes shall dwell—
Home of my fathers, fare thee well!

Thy sunny banks, thy murmuring rills,
  Where music, oft my heart hath cheered,
Thy flowery lawns, thy verdant hills,
  Still to this bosom are endeared;
Fond memory on thy scenes shall dwell,
Home of my fathers, fare thee well!

The warbling birds, that sweetly sang
  At morn, around my fav'rite tree,—
The merry bells, that loudly rang,
  How dear their mem'ry still to me;
May peace within thy bosom dwell,
Land of my fathers, fare thee well!

Yet dearer still the peaceful cot,
   Where parents lov'd, and friends caressed,
Within thy walls, oh! lovely spot,
   May heaven's rich blessings ever rest:
My memory on thy scenes shall dwell,
Home of my fathers, fare thee well!

MY MOTHER'S GRAVE.

THERE is a spot I love to tread,
   At midnight's peaceful hour,
When sinks the sun beneath the west,
   And closed is every flower.

When not a ripple doth appear,
   To wake the slumbering wave,
Oh! then I love to sit and weep
   Beside my mother's grave.

When nature, from her slumbers wakes,
   To hail the opening morn,
I love to kiss the clay cold turf
   That wraps her gentle form.

Though doom'd to meet the cruel storm,
   On life's tempestuous wave,
One spot shall still be dear to me,
   My mother's lonely grave.

IDA;

TELL me, ye glittering hosts of light,
   That nightly gem yon arch above,
If in your beauteous realms so bright,
   She dwells, the sister of my love.
Her lute unstrung, neglected lies—
   No more its chords her fingers sweep,—
Far from her own fair Grecian skies,
   She in her lonely grave doth sleep.
Ye birds that round this wild retreat,
   Warble your notes from bough to bough,
To me your music once was sweet,
   But, oh! it only mocks me now.
All nature smiles, but not for me;
   And at my feet her flow'rets bloom;
Yet while their opening buds I see,
   It o'er me casts a deeper gloom.

'Tis wrong—but, oh ! I cannot bear,
  While she in death is sleeping here,
That aught she lov'd a smile should wear.
  Oh, lost Ianthe ! sister dear,
How my sad spirit longs to break
  Its earthly chain, and soar away,
Where angel choirs harmonious wake
  In heavenly strains their choral lay.
My bosom's idol is no more ;
  I have no tie to bind me here ;
I would that on our native shore,
  Thou did'st repose, my sister dear.
Oh, Greece ! my own bright land of song,
  To thee my eager fancy strains ;
Before me rise a youthful throng,
  Companions of my childhood's days ;
Land where the muses lov'd to dwell—
Land of the cypress ! "fare thee well."

Thus Ida mus'd ; the shades of night
  Were gathering round a lonely wood,
Where in a simple robe of white,
  Beside a new made grave she stood.
Her eye was of the mildest blue,
  But its bright glance had pass'd away,
And with her curls of auburn hue,
  The sporting zephyrs seemed to play.
She could not weep, or for the grief
  That weigh'd so heavy on her heart,

She might have found that sweet relief,
　Which falling tears alone impart.
One hand upon her brow was press'd,
　As on her knees she sank in prayer;
The other held, with fond caress,
　A ringlet of her sister's hair.
"Father, divine," she meekly said,
　"Oh! deign to hear the suppliant's prayer;
On me thy chastening hand is laid;
　I ask for strength, my grief to bear."
She rose, and in her tearless eye,
　A look of calm submission beam'd—
She rais'd it to the azure sky,
　Where night's pale lamp all lovely gleam'd;
Then parting from her snowy brow,
　The tresses that were waving there,
Upon a mound, herself she threw,
　Fann'd by the cool refreshing air.
She rais'd her deep blue eyes once more,
　Her hands were clasp'd upon her breast,
One gentle sigh, and all was o'er—
　The broken-hearted was at rest.

Farewell, Grecian maiden! thy grief-stricken
　　bosom,
　No longer convulsive with agony heaves;
A grave by the side of thy sister we've made thee,
　And pity, a sigh o'er thy memory breathes.

M*

We'll plant near thy pillow the cypress and
    myrtle ;
  The willow shall weep o'er thy desolate grave,
The rose and the woodbine, shall blossom around
    thee,—
  Farewell, Grecian maiden ! fair child of the
    brave.

PSALM IV. 8.

"I will both lay me down in peace, and sleep: for thou,
Lord, only, makest me to dwell in safety."

DRAWN is the curtain of the night,
   Oh! 't is the sacred hour of rest;
Sweet hour, I hail thee with delight,
   Thrice welcome to my weary breast.

Oh, God! to thee, my fervent prayer,
   I offer, kneeling at thy feet;
Tho' humbly breath'd, oh! deign to hear—
   Smile on me from the mercy seat.

While angels round, their watches keep,
   Whose harps thy praise unceasing swell,
"I lay me down in peace, and sleep,"
   For thou in safety mak'st me dwell.

Drawn is the curtain of the night—
   Thou bid'st creation silent be—
And now, with holy, calm delight,
   Father, I would commune with thee.

Shepherd of Israel, deign to keep,
   And guard my soul from every ill;
Thus will I lay me down, and sleep,
   For thou in safety mak'st me dwell.

THE CHRISTMAS HYMN.

How tranquil, how serene the night,
 When to the sleeping earth,
A heavenly host of seraphs bright,
 Proclaim'd a Saviour's birth !

The shepherds, on Judea's plains,
 With wonder heard their songs,
" Glory to God !—to Him alone,
 Our highest praise belongs."

" Glory to God !" through heaven's broad arch,
 The sacred chorus ran,
Good will, and never-ending peace,
 Henceforth to mortal man.

" Glory to God !" let all the earth,
 To Him their honours bring,
And every heart, and every tongue,
 His praise responsive sing.

TO SOLITUDE.

I LOVE at twilight's pensive hour,
   To hie me to some lonely spot,
Where dew-drops kiss each sleeping flower,
   And daily toil and cares forgot.

Fain would I trace each lingering star,
   That glistens in yon cloudless sky,—
They shed their radiant beams afar,
   But dawn not on the sightless eye.

Yet solitude has charms for me,
   Oh ! how I love its lone retreat ;
The breeze that whispers through each tree,
   Steals on my ear like music sweet.

I love the laving stream to hear,
   Meandering through the valley fair ;
But there's a joy more sweet, more dear,
   The gentle *muse* inspires me there.

Borne on its wings, my spirit flies,
　Far, far beyond terrestrial spheres ;
To planetary worlds I rise,
　While distant music glads my ears.

What are the festive halls of mirth,
　Oh, solitude ! compared with thee ?
The purest, brightest spots of earth,
　Are thy sequestered wilds to me.

THE BLIND GIRL'S SONG.

THEY tell me of a sunny sky,
  Tinged with etherial light ;
But, ah ! for me, no sunbeams shine,
  My day is veil'd in night.

Yet, there's a beam, a nobler beam,
  Of knowledge, bright and fair ;
That beam may light my darken'd path,
  And soften every care.

The moon that o'er the sleeping earth,
  Shines forth in majesty,
The sparkling deep that proudly rolls,
  Hath no delights for me.

Yet I can hear a brother's voice,
  In tenderest accents speak ;
And feel a sister's pearly tear,
  Steal gently on my cheek.

"SHALL I MEET THEE AGAIN?"

DEDICATED TO A FELLOW PUPIL IN THE INSTITUTION.

SHALL I meet thee again, where so oft we
    have met,
  When our bosoms from sorrow were free?
Oh, those moments of pleasure will steal o'er me
    yet,
  When thou art far distant from me!

Shall I meet thee again, 'neath the green wil-
    low's shade,
  That waves o'er Oneida's calm lake?
When the mild rays of evening in loveliness fade,
  Shall my lute, its soft music awake?

Oh! say shall I meet thee unalter'd again—
  Thy friendship as fervent as now?
Or will absence efface from thy bosom my name,
  And cold be the smile on thy brow?

JERUSALEM.

I STOOD upon the mount, called Olivet,
The spot where once the blessed Saviour sat ;
And from his lips divinely flow'd
Accents of mercy, to a fallen race.
The sun had sunk beneath the crimson west,
And night, around its dusky mantle threw.
All—all was still—and as mine eyes survey'd
The ruins of that city, once so fair,
I wept ; and half unconscious, from my lips,
Broke forth these scattered thoughts.—

Jerusalem !
How like that glorious orb, thou once wert lovely!
But, alas ! how changed thy glory is !
A night of deeper gloom enshrouds thee now.
Here once, magnificent, a temple stood,
And Israel's God was worshipped and adored ;
But where that temple now ? Oh, not one stone
Is left, to mark the spot where once it stood.
Jehovah's name, by heathen lips blasphemed,
And Israel, once a mighty nation strong,
O'er all the earth dispersed—a scattered few—

Shunned, and despised, alas! in exile roam ;
Ill-fated city, 't was thy crimes alone,
That hurl'd upon thy head this misery !

"Would thou had'st known, in thy prosperity,
The things that to thy peace belonged !
But now, they from thine eyes are hid :"
Oh ! thou hast slain the Lord's anointed Saviour
    of thy race !
And thou hast said, " His blood on us, and on
    our children be."
Yet, there is hope for *thee*, Jerusalem !
Weep o'er thy sins, and to thy God return ;
Believe Messiah has already come,
And plead the merits of his pardoning blood.

ADDRESS,

Delivered May, 1843, at the N. Y. Tabernacle, at the Anniversary Exhibition of the Pupils of the New York Institution for the Blind.

THEY tell us of the starry train,
  That sparkles in yon sky of blue,
When gently o'er the verdant plain
  Mild evening sheds its pensive hue.

And of the glorious orb of day,
  That 'lames the spacious earth we tread;
But vain, alas, its golden ray
  Upon our sightless eye is shed.

They tell us of the landscape fair,
  The gushing fount—the pleasant shade—
Of spring's young flowers that blossom there,
  In nature's lovely garb arrayed.

The smile that decks the human face—
  The brilliant eye—the joyous brow,—
Are beauties we may never trace—
  A rayless midnight shrouds us now.

But why, ah! why, the falling tear?
  Why heaves the sad unbidden sigh?
The lamp of knowledge, bright and fair,
  Pours lustre on our mental eye.

And oh! Religion's heavenly ray,
  Our bosoms light with sacred love,
And bids us look from earth away,
  To an eternal world above.

To us our Father hath denied
  The blessings he on you bestows,
Yet, sweetly now our moments glide—
  He gives us friends to soothe our woes.

And oh! we never can express
  The gratitude to you we owe—
God your benevolence shall bless,
  And his approving smile bestow.

AN ADDRESS,

DELIVERED BY FRANCES JANE CROSBY, A PUPIL OF THE
NEW YORK INSTITUTION FOR THE BLIND,

At the Hall of the House of Representatives, in presence of
the Senate and Representatives of the United States, on
the occasion of an exhibition given by seventeen pupils
from the Institution, at Washington, January 24, 1844.

Our Union's Capitol! fair Washington—
Thou bear'st the father of thy country's name!
A hero, whose illustrious deeds have won
Triumphant laurels of undying fame.

That soul, alive to every generous flame,
None ever ask'd his sympathy in vain;
That noble hero sleeps, and o'er his grave,
See freedom's spangled banner proudly wave!

Peace to the ashes of the mighty dead!
Who in the glorious cause of freedom bled:
Methinks that now, from yonder starry sphere,
Their guardian spirits hover o'er you here.

N*

Dear friends, a sightless group presumes to claim
Your kind attention, not, we trust, in vain ;
A sister State is ours, her fostering care,
Yes, her benevolence we largely share.

As o'er the mighty Hudson's breast you fly,
A stately edifice attracts your eye ;
That edifice our generous State has rear'd,
Our happy home, long to our hearts endear'd.

Ah! yes, 't was there our fingers learn'd to trace,
The sacred volume, God's own word of grace ;
Kind friends watch o'er us with parental care,
Our every joy, our every grief they share.

What though these orbs in rayless darkness roll,
Instruction pours its radiance o'er the soul,
And fancy pictures to the mental eye,
The glittering hosts that 'lume the midnight sky.

The noble strains of music, sweet and clear,
You have this evening heard, were taught us
        there ;
Where time its rapid flight unheeded wings,
Each fleeting moment some new pleasure brings.

Oh, you who here from every State convene,
Illustrious band ! may we not hope the scene

You now behold, will prove to every mind,
Instruction hath a ray to cheer the blind.

Without that ray, sad were indeed their lot,
Dejected, lonely, and too oft forgot,—
They brood in silent sadness o'er their woe,
For them our tears of heartfelt pity flow.

One boon of you, illustrious band! we claim,
Oh! say our boon shall not be ask'd in vain;
Go aid their cause, and rear for them a home,
Leave, leave them not unheeded still to roam.

Go aid their cause, their mental night dispel,
Bid grief's sad sigh no more their bosoms swell;
May every State in this bright land of fame,
An *Institution for the Blind* contain.

Go aid their cause, and He who reigns above,
Will your kind labours graciously approve;
Those sightless ones, your tender cares relieve,
For you full many a grateful prayer will breathe.

AN ADDRESS,

DELIVERED BY FRANCES JANE CROSBY, A PUPIL, ETC.,

Before the Governor, Council and Assembly of the State of
New Jersey, on the occasion of an exhibition given before
that body, at Trenton, by twenty pupils from the Institution.   January 29, 1844.

Now mid the evening sky serene,
Majestic rolls night's silver queen ;
Her starry train revolving round,
Smiles o'er calm nature's sleep profound.

Alas ! though mild their lustre be,
Their beauties we may never see ;
But there 's a ray more pure, more bright,
That in our bosoms sheds its light.

That ray our darken'd path beguiles,
And wreaths the clouded brow with smiles ;
'T is education, dearer far
Than brilliant moon, or beaming star.

Thanks to our Father, God above,
For the rich tokens of his love ;
The blind girl's home he deigns to bless,
And turns her grief to happiness.

How oft, at evening's silent hour,
When zephyrs fan each fragrant flower,
And peaceful nature calmly slept
In pensive sadness, we have wept.

Now sweetly glide the hours away,
Cheered by soft music's thrilling ray ;
And pure affection's accents dear,
Fall gently on our listening ear.

We—honor'd legislative band !
With glowing hearts before you stand ;—
We plead for those bereft of sight,
Who sigh for education's light.

We tender you our thanks sincere,
For those entrusted to our care ;
But many, *many* yet remain,
And shall we plead for them in vain ?

TO HIS EXCELLENCY, THE GOVERNOR.

We, honor'd sir! appeal to thee,
In their behalf—thy sympathy
We humbly ask—thou, ever kind,
Will not refuse to aid the blind.

To say, we are aware 't is thine,*
On whom instruction's light may shine;
And will this generous State deny,
The fund sufficient to supply

Those, who their aid, their pity claim;
And must we plead for them in vain?
No, honor'd sir! this must not be;
Once more we ask thy sympathy.

Make them the objects of thy care,
May they the light of knowledge share;
And many a prayer for thee will rise,
To Him enthroned above the skies.

---

* Referring to the act empowering the Governor to nomi-
nate the subjects for instruction under its provisions.

ADDRESS,

Recited at several exhibitions when on a tour through the western part of the State of New York, in August, 1842, inviting the public to send the Blind to the Institution.

CONTENTED, happy, tho' a sightless band,
Dear friends! this evening we before you stand;
We for a moment your attention claim,
And trust that boon will not be asked in vain.

The varied scenes the rural landscape yields,
The smiling meadows and the flowery fields,
The boundless Ocean and the vaulted skies,
Must never, never glad these sightless eyes.

But there's a lamp within, whose sacred light,
Burns with a lustre ever pure and bright—
'Tis education—we have shown to you
What by its rays illumed, the blind can do.

Without it, life a dreary waste would be,
With nought to break its long monotony;
No sunny beams to light our cheerless way—
Our vacant thoughts, ah! whither would they
     stray!

But thanks to God, his sovereign care we own,
He hath not left us friendless and alone,—
His pitying eye beheld the helpless blind,
And reared us friends affectionate and kind.

Fain would I bear you to our happy home—
Come then with me, on fancy's pinions roam,
Where peace and love, twin sisters, fondly smile,
And music's strains our cheerless hours beguile.

When fair Aurora from the orient sky
Bids night's celestial orb before her fly,
We hail the opening day with vigor new,
And with delight our various tasks pursue.

But oh! while thus our moments sweetly glide,
We think of those like us of sight denied,
Whose minds, enshrouded in a mental night,
Sigh to behold instruction's glorious light.

Perchance some tender parent now is here,
Whose only child, perhaps a daughter dear,
Of sight bereaved, doth tears of pity claim,
Then why at home that darling one detain?

Place, I entreat you, place your offspring there,
Where she the blessings we enjoy may share;
Where, pruned by education's culturing hand,
Her intellect, long dormant, may expand.

And she will bless you with affection's tears,
When she to you returns in after years—
Will with her fingers trace the sacred page,
When o'er you steals apace declining age.

AN ADDRESS,

Composed and recited while on a tour with a party from the Institution through the interior of the State of New York, in September, 1843.

THE deep blue sky, serenely bright,
   On which your eyes with rapture gaze ;
Where stars unveil their mellow light,
   And God his wondrous power displays :

The gushing fount, whose glassy breast,
   Reflects the parting hues of day,
Nature, in robes of verdure drest,
   The opening buds, the flow'rets gay ;

The lofty hills, the greenwood bowers,—
   Though fair these rural scenes appear,
On them to gaze must ne'er be ours ;
   These orbs, alas! they cannot cheer.

But, oh! instruction's nobler light,
   Sheds on our mental eye its ray ;
We hail its beams with new delight,
   And bid each gloomy thought away.

To us, our God kind friends has given,
　　Whose names we ever shall revere;
Recorded in the book of heaven,
　　Shall their munificence appear.

'T was they who reared the happy home,
　　Beneath whose peaceful roof we dwell;
No more unheeded now we roam,
　　Our lips the notes of gladness swell.

But while our sunny moments fly,
　　Unsullied by a shade of care,
For those like us bereft, we sigh,
　　And wish they, too, our joys might share.

Is there no tender parent here,
　　Who oft in sorrow weeps alone,
For the sweet child he holds so dear,
　　O'er whom a rayless night is thrown?

Then place amid our youthful band,
　　That lov'd one, cherish'd long by thee;
There will her intellect expand,
　　And her young heart beat light and free.

There will her fingers learn to trace
　　The page by inspiration given;—
The page of sacred truth and grace—
　　The star that guides her soul to heaven.